FROM MUD TO HOUSE

A Photo Essay
by Bertram T. Knight

Children's Press

A Division of Grolier Publishing
New York London Hong Kong Sydney
Danbury, Connecticut

Created and Developed by The Learning Source

Designed by Josh Simons

Acknowledgments: We would like to thank the Cherokee Environmental Group, and the Brick Association of North Carolina for their time, effort, and help with this book. Special thanks goes to Betty Potter of the Brick Institute of America, for without her this book would not have been possible.

Photo Credits: Acme Brick Company: 27; Paul & Shirley Berquist: 8, 9 (right); Brick Association of North Carolina: cover (inset), 2, 17 (inset), 22, 31; Brick Institute of America: 1, 6, 7, 9 (left), 11 (top), 13, 14, 15, 16-17, 18, 20, 24, 25, 26, 28, 29, 30 (inset), back cover; Cherokee Environmental Group: cover (background), 10, 11 (bottom), 12, 19, 21, 23; Ken Karp: 30; Tom & Pat Leeson: 5 (top); Lynn M. Stone: 5 (bottom); SuperStock: 3, 4.

Note: The actual brickmaking process often varies from manufacturer to manufacturer. The process described in this book is representative of one of the most common methods of making bricks today.

Library of Congress Cataloging-in-Publication Data
Knight, Bertram T.
      From mud to house : a photo essay / by Bertram T. Knight.
      p. cm. -- (Changes)
      Summary: Describes how imporant bricks are, where they come from, how they are made, and what people build with them.
    ISBN 0-516-20737-7 (lib.bdg.)   0-516-20365-7 (pbk.)
      1. Brickmaking--Juvenile literature. 2. Building, Brick--Juvenile literature.
[1. Brickmaking. 2. Bricks.] I. Title. II Series: Changes (New York, N.Y.)
TP828.K55 1997
666'.737--dc21   97-23609
                                            CIP
                                            AC

Printed in the United States of America.
1 2 3 4 5 6 7 8 9 10 R 06 05 04 03 02 01 00 99 98 97

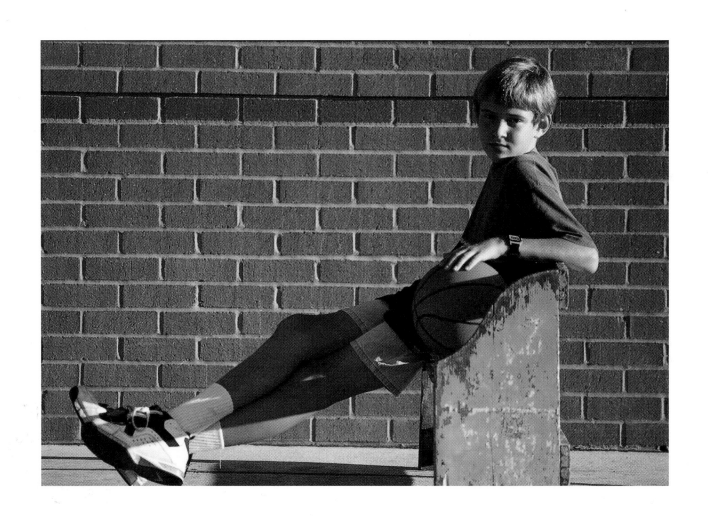

Riddle: What did the ancient Egyptians have in common with the three little pigs and the big, bad wolf?

The answer is **brick**. They all discovered what we know today—that for homes, schools, office buildings, and more—nothing is stronger than brick.

After all, it can stand up to any kind of weather or even a raging fire.

But where does brick come from?

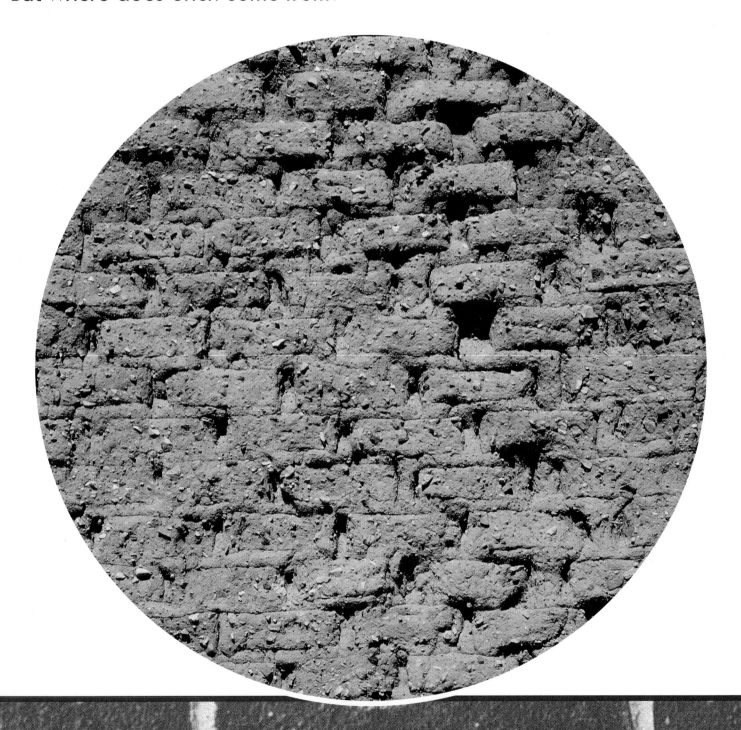

For thousands of years, desert people have been making brick out of mud mixed with sand, clay, straw, and sometimes grass. The muddy mix is then dried by the sun and cut into building blocks called adobe.

Today's brick, too, comes from mud. But the mud is now made of clay mined from the earth.

After mighty bulldozers pull the clay from the ground . . .

. . . workers test it for quality. The very best will be used for making bricks.

The clay goes to a storehouse . . .

. . . and then to a crushing machine. Here, huge grinding wheels smash the clay again and again.

Next, mesh screens sift the clay back and forth. Only the smallest pieces are able to pass through. Chunks and lumps go back for more crushing.

The sifted powder then waits in mountainlike piles. Little by little, it is scooped up and mixed with water to make a stiff, smooth mud.

Now a forming die, or mold, shapes the mud into long rectangular columns called ribbons.

At the same time, holes are cut through the center of each ribbon. This makes the bricks lighter in weight.

Then a special machine cuts the ribbon into separate bricks.

Stacked high on carts, the bricks pass through a long warming room called a tunnel dryer. Once the bricks are dry they are ready for firing.

The bricks now go into a huge kiln. This is a very, very hot oven about the length of a football field. Inside, the bricks are baked and hardened.

It takes a while for the bricks to pass through the kiln. Afterward, they are moved into the open and allowed to cool to room temperature.

Later, row upon row of new bricks fill the warehouse.

As orders come in, the bricks are stacked on wooden platforms. Forklifts load them onto trucks.

Soon, they will be delivered into the hands of people . . .

. . . who build the strong, beautiful brick structures
that we all use . . .

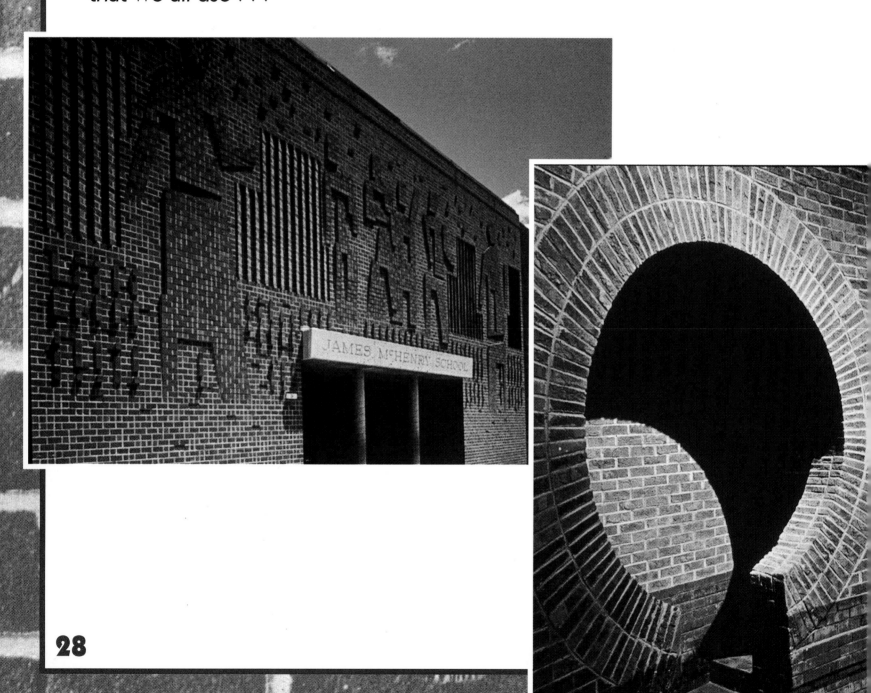

. . . for working . . .

. . . for playing . . .

and for learning new things, such as . . .

. . . how bricks are made!

Here are some examples of brick patterns. Can you find any of them near your home or school?

Running Bond

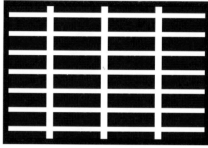

Stack Bond

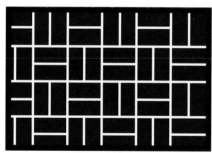

Basket Weave

Flemish Bond

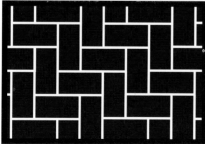

Herringbone

English Bond